For Val Sutherland

FYRISH

by

Bryan Walters

Rainbow Books, 171 Victoria Road, Aberdeen AB1 3ND

First published 1st September 1975

Cover design by Val Sutherland, Stewart Cordiner

Printed by Rainbow Enterprises, 171 Victoria Road, Aberdeen.

CONTENTS

SEEN BUT NOT SCENERY

(Memo to town and country planners)

The valley is a lead-lined vault,
preserved against time,

yet so soon it could be turned
into a grave that's robbed by man -

Filled with multi-coloured caravans -
Clearly seen, but not scenery.

BOY IN AMETHYST   (for Brian Langtry)
(at Llywernog Mining Museum, Ponterwyd)

A child,
three years of age perhaps,
eyes still dry from a distant laugh,
yelled piercingly.

His father,
face inscrutable as the miner
on the photograph,
held on - ignored the noise,
sought for something new
to peer into,
hoping it would go away,
like thunder does.

His mother,
pregnant with another yell, walked in,
'My poor deprived child' intoned.
The sarcasm was lost on one compelled
to seek attention in this noisy fashion.
So, he yelled again.
Inevitably he won -
They went, unwilling to endure
the strain of his persistent,
and determined wish,
to have his own will done.

Nearby, a boy
was fascinated by a polished stone
of mauve.
Carefully, he replaced it on its wooden stand,
turned round with eyes reflecting
all the wonder found in amethyst,
and walked away, ...alone.

8

BECAUSE OF HEIGHT

Those few remaining bones,
marrow-less, flame-charred;
dusted with the accumulations
of four thousand years
beneath the wind-worn summit shale
of Disgwylfa Fawr.

The red hair,
surviving death's transfiguration
and the pigment-bleaching light;
a final couching deep within
the confines of a tree,
hewn down and hollowed out
to hold the spiritless remains
of some ancient Celtic chief.

They are far away (the bones)
in Cardiff now, carelessly heaped
in a grey clay vessel,
whitened by the cold, white,
shadow-resisting Museum light,
far from the saucered cyst,
and safe from the clumsy incisions
of hunting men,
unaware of their own tumours.

Walking in that misty mausoleum,
I think I hear a requiem,
stretched to monosyllables
by the heathen wind -
a mere stutter in memoriam.

Respectfully, I replace a single stone,
then pass by humbly,
scarcely comprehending more than
the distant 'hurry-by',
but because of height,
closer to the sky . . . .

RHEIDOL

(The River and its human counterpart : seven facets)

You will not live long -
Your father flung short sharp rain
into the hooded hill from his scudding frenzy.
You absorbed his morbid tendency,
and wilfully wounded those with weaker ways.

Insensitively and in formative days,
you set your destiny; challenged the world;
hurled yourself headlong downhill.
You speak volubly, but the world will have its say.

You thought you knew it all, but see,
a barrier so tall that even your impertinent course
is halted. You are forced to change your ways;
enter the door that others draw you through
in channelled order.

Resilient and militant, bursting now within;
filled with hatred for authority, and careless
of conformity, you thrust your way through hollowed wombs,
and with climactic lunge, you plunge
into a new environment where two thoughts
merge as one.

You lose your head -
Turned by the glow and glitter of synthetic stars,
you find yourself entrapped by worldliness
that once lapped at your lording feet.
Confused, your built-up dreams seem
but a stilled reflection of your former self.
What you willed is thwarted and lies
lengthways on a shelf of rock.

You are broken -
In a sort of shattered determination
you wind and wander in a stupor of reluctant defeat.
You progress, yet you find yourself
in embarrassing retreat.

Although you storm beneath,
the pattern of flow is set by time,
and those who thrust ahead will blunt a nose!
Your headstrong youth must conform
to the populous ocean. What once made you
distinctly different, is lost now in the mediocrity
of recurring themes . . . . If you doubt,
return to the source of short sharp rain
and look down on the sea.
Now tell me - What did you attain?
You ended up the same!

BLIND JOHN

'Don't you ever lose that walking stick'
she always said. How could
he ever forget his mind's
antenna - The extended limb of wood

lovingly gloss-whitened by his mother,
not so much for the purpose
of being seen, but rather
to be recognised as blind, like lepers

used to carry warning bells - He never
knew just how white, was white. Only
knew a world where various
sounds were shades of light, and to be lonely

meant the silence of insistent night,
indoors; a clear, bright-mooned
night, when closed windows shut out
the crackle of frost, and ears, attuned

to perfect pitch, to note a faulty reed
on his accordion; identify
the higher octaves of a bat,
could only hear the symmetry

of fear revolving deep within his
sightless head - So, John became
a busker . . . . Accordion, old haversack,
and cloth collecting bag in which he claimed

the wherewithal to travel between towns,
discovering new sounds, the scraping
of strange footpaths, the unexpected hand,
the changing accents - Ever alert for chink

of copper; cupro-nickel; then a nod
of thanks. For six determined years
of thrusting sounds at sounds,
combined with the acuteness of his ears'

touch, enabled John to keep his independence -
Then one cold January night, he 'phoned
his home, tapped his way down
Cardiff's neon streets, ice-boned

and weary for the crowds that stayed
at home on that inclement day.
No more was heard of John for many months,
until two men investigated what they

thought was gas escaping from a damaged pipe
beneath the derelict Tredegar Arms -
There, crouched against the cellar wall,
they found Blind John, his palms

still clasping his collecting bag with
seven pounds and fourteen pence inside.
'I know it is my John' his mother said,
'I painted that stick so many times, I recognised

the marks on it'. But no one could
determine, from what remained
the questions and the scars that Blind John carried
through his thirty years, unanswered, unexplained.

THE ORIGINAL FIELD

He was once a field
    wild with flowers.
No plough had ever despoiled
    the ragged pattern
of wind-blown seeds,
    slowly seeding towards
the deep repeating stream.
    Then a worming spirocete
had spread a progeny of spores,
    consuming every fibre
of his natural wilderness.

The day I walked
    into the furrowed sterility
of the city asylum,
    I saw no flowers
growing in his gates.
    A grey mist obscured
his hollows,
    and the wind
was stilled below a word.

So easy to deny
    the original field,
I thought,
    until his son walked in.

'AND WHO CAN MEASURE PAIN?'

The wind is two wings wide
measured by the outstretched span
of the soaring forked tail Kite.

With strong encircling arms, I can
hold my dark girl tight.
Who can measure the love I feel inside?

ENGLYN TO A MONOLITH

Observing the single stone, leaning on
the harsh wind's monotone,
I understand why we soon
forget memories of our own.

GRAVEYARD GATE

(an Englyn)

Withered woman, drooping head, selling flowers,
their petals about to shed;
a bouquet presented;
the dying for the dead.

IN THIS YOUR COUNTRY SLEEP

(For Aeronwy Thomas-Ellis on the occasion of her
appearance at the Abbey Theatre, Dublin, 10th June '74.)
To the memory of Dylan Thomas . . . .

Can you look out and see
in what would be your sixtieth year
to questionable heaven,
the herons, gulls, rooks and rain ;
hear again the town awake to wringing wind?

Can you comprehend still
the singing of a heart-sought truth
on your eminent higher hill ?
Answer me from the knowledge in ageing lines -
Can a child joy, and die three times?

You realised that joy
is the knock of dust ; the rusting tower ;
the leaning scene ; the action's end.
You stood tip-toe, shouted at the moon
and storm, sea-bed and shore -
Asserted the authority of the sun.
Yet I suspect that you, the inner man,
did surely know that death
would have the ultimate dominion.

You felt the time of No Time -
Heard the Bells of No God -
And, eyelids heavy with copper,
doubted the breaking dawn.
Them torn by the lot, unbid,
but knocked down by the One who shatters light,
you told your riding girl not to fear,
to wake each day ; believe that death
is not a violation of the law,
only a turning of the earth each wounding year.

18

And here today, faithed in the leaping saga
of prayer, believing in the brimming words,
stands a daughter whose roots are fused in green,
fresh from the field of telling lines,
green with green,
and first in voice from another world.

Is this your answer then,
spoken from a distant shore?

Like Drumcliff's stone
you leaned and fell,
were carved again from newest sky.
'What then?' is what is now,
and lives in Lapis Lazuli.

LOVE SPOONS

He remembered her
as she was -
Kept the memories
precious as porcelain and wood,
hung and meticulously placed
in perfect composition,
just as she would have done.

They always did dwell in the past,
grasped Victoriana when they could,
copper kettle, brass spittoon,
candle-sticks, mahogany wood
oval table, chairs to match.
Crown Derby plates and Coalport cups,
engravings framed in Hogarth
black and gold, after exceptions,
five to be exact. A lithograph,
bought from an exhibition,
of a nude reclining in the afternoon,
and four love spoons,
knife-notched from oak so old
that hours of carving worked the wood
before the objects could be sold
to them in Wales, brought back,
and hung upon emulsioned walls.

They parted.

Three years passed.

Compulsively she must return to view
the opportunity that she had lost.
She came at night, the red glow
on the walls, the beams of black,
the wine in candlelight; attempted
to renew the visions of the past.
But that is where they stayed,

for he had since known other girls,
collected other curios,
kept them locked elsewhere.

He knew her price -
He knew her worth,
resented her audacity.
He would not pay -
She did not stay,
his memories he preferred;
the memories she had brought to birth,
stillborn as the verb to love, with pain.

The spoons,
he had discovered with a closer look,
were carved against the grain.

LOVE IN SECRET

(after Dafydd ap Gwilym)

(one)

Dafydd - Your love in secret
was a summer love . . . .
Walking and worshipping beneath the candles;
the candlesticks of silver birch trees.
Your altar moss - Pillowed moss.

I too have lingered in the longer grass;
watched the twitching of the light side
of the leaves against the blue and white;
walked the high moors with my hair-strewn girl,
excited by the lyre of the sudden grouse.

(two)

It is winter now -
Our summer is revolving round another sun.
I sit in the high-winged chair,
but cannot contain the draught
around my outstretched feet.
I point my empty glass towards
the fairy-lighted Christmas tree;
look down the stem;
          attempt to turn the earth;
See through a myriad whirling galaxies
of light and try to conjure up the Southern Cross,
but vexed with fate, can only grope.
The swinging bauble of the night eludes my grasp,
and lying shattered on the floor,
unwittingly becomes a symbol of my hope.

(three)

The conifers comb the long dark rushing air
  of the night around my mountain home -
      You who lie asleep
      at the waist of the wind,

Listen!
It is not the wind you hear
that cries.

(four)
Words steal too easily
from the heart,
slip into a line ;
are guarded by a question mark.

(five)
Hidden love
is like a mole beneath the turf.
It is blind,
but all can see its work.

I'll say no more . . . .

CURIOSITY

Accidents draw forth crowds
and comments.

The bar conversation was accidents.
An off-duty policeman told of
the dead cyclist;
the curious crowd;
the severed leg in a field;
the wedge of glass in the head;
a faceless body;
protruding bones;
crushed skulls.

In a corner sat three men;
bent; hands on knees;
staring blankly at
    the floor . . . .
       the empty fire . . . .
          nothing . . . .

A thin pale mouth stabbed
at the backs of the bar tenders . . . . .

'I fought at . . . . . .'

His words limped.
His tongue lolled,
and a solitary red poppy
rolled out and fell into the dust -

The crowd
          stopped talking

and looked
        curiously

SPIDER

'All right boyo :
So, you're on the wall
and I'm in bed -
The light disturbs you?
Sorry! I know it's late
but I can't sleep.

You don't know what it's like to feel trapped
do you?
Never been a fly!

Big wall isn't it?

No bookshelves   No windows

No curtains   No pictures

Just a great big empty world of white emulsion

Reckon you've got your problems though.

Look now! You've fallen.
Know why?
You've got no hang up boyo,
and you haven't even got the feet of a fly'.

CATKINS

Sometimes
 you hang like
 dried catkins
 on my memory
once
 you were new
 swaying green
 against the blue sky
even
 in the summer storm
 you clung
 to your silver form
when
 the winds blades
 tore tinged and
 shook you stayed
then
 touched by a single
 snowflake you shrunk
 and mingled
 with a greyed
 and withered stem
sometimes
 i remember you
 as new catkins
 an old
 and dried memory
 i cannot accept
 fight hard to reject
 the seasons
 of both you
 and them
 but seldom win

INDIAN SUMMER

Once we were plentiful on the vast plains;
hunted the fiery prairies,
and stalked the scrubbed canyons.

> We lay in the red hills;
> smoked the pipe of peace,
> and adored our totems.

Through many suns and moons we rode;
learned the ways of the wild,
and gathered fruits from the forest's lip.

> We understood each other's signals;
> puzzled the sky with secret messages.
> The years grew tender beneath our consciousness.

Then storms blew across the face of our land.
Gritty sand billowed and howled.
Our spirits fled, and the hills were obscured.

> In the darkness, we hunted each other.
> Our silent talk
> was blown to unknown threats.

We hid ourselves;
tried to shelter in our own shadows.
In our confusion, we rode with others.

> You settled
> beneath distant hills and a strange sky -
> Your rivers are controlled,
> and you have your reservations.

But I prefer the frightened wind of the evening rites;
the rituals of rock-channelled torrents;
new summits,
and the prancing mare in red heat.

> You
> ride in rapidly diminishing circles.
> I
> in a circle that has no end.

FYRISH
(for Val)

Distanced by four hundred miles,
you ask me now to touch you - hold you.
Hold you, as on that last locked night
in the owl-sounding hills,
close and wordless,
until soon after dawn
the cuckoo slipped from wire to wire
mocking the meadow-pipit.
And the curlew forsook its 'coorlie'
for a warbling invitation to a mate.

We didn't wake to them -
We never slept!
Then from that hushed chapter
of breathing spirit,
as on that fifth distant day,
when God formed sounds other than
the rushing wind and water,
came that two-syllabled clarity
that thrust the fledgling
from the nest of night.

Knowing you would soon be gone,
I held you then particularly tight -
Drew back the curtains -
Watched your eyes fill
with the brimming light
that dabbled on the whitened pine above -
Then held you next to me, around me
and within me with a ferocity and intensity
that sought to deny the gravity
of whatever drew you far away -
four hundred miles . . . .

And now tonight, you ask me, will I hold you?
Hold you on an impulse through a wire?

Cariad, I'll stay awake,
until the sky is lightened with a greenish hue,
So listen to the sounds that come with day's first fire
(so many millions of miles away),
and find me there, close there, alongside you.

LOCH MHOR

You are solitary as the ghostly
      roe deer in fear of breath.
Sudden snipe arrow in a fling of wing -
beats. From crazed mud, fossil footprints take flight,
      and light lie the hollowed bones
of the sheep, gnawed by the shore's teeth of death.

You are a mystical pool of moon flare ;
      bats tangle in your night air,
and owls pipe to the tune called by the breeze
and taut trees. You crease when clouds wrap the moon ;
      fold when wind writhes in your lap.
The deer, stiffening, sniffs the air, aware

in the texture of scents, the spectre of
      man who haunts the gaunt moor's
edge from the blind eyes of a deserted
stone wedge. Bleached tree stumps, leached by bog, are stark,
      spectral, ancestral ; only
lone skeletons survive your claw, Loch Mhor !

GULL
(for Mark)

You laugh
as the yapping
dog
sets in flight
the white as foam
and yellow-beak
shell-seeking
gull.

You gently feel
a flat and grey-worn
stone
smoothed by the ocean's wide
and sand-grained
tongue.

It slides
into your pocket,
whereas the wild gull
sidles
on the water's
soft and chequered
cloth.

VOICE OF THE GODS
(Stockholm 1975)

Eighteen floors
of students' rooms
have flawed
Valhallavägen.

The gods appear
to those who would
look down,
not up.

Emerging
from the snows of March,
and rooted in the rockery,
a yellow coltsfoot
claws its way to light,
and opens wide in mockery.

TRANSPARENT BLACK   (for Dannie Abse)

I remember the real black.
The day I walked
through the slack wind,
when the clouds were anchored
to the ground by chains of smoke,
and a yellow claw,
not from the pollen of columbine,
but sulphured
by the vulturing descent of chemicals,
talloned the lungs
and tore at the jaundiced eyes.

That day,
the train knew scars of soot
on windows emptied of view,
until the leaves of Worcestershire
swallowed up the manufactured spores,
and took me where, with rod and line,
I happily caught a breath, no more.

Today, I ventured back.
No eyesore plumes of smoke were seen.
Instead I smelled the fumes, transparent black,
and wished I'd never been.

NOISE

Half past midnight -
Saturday night's noise
goes home -
Your river
bed is comfortable -
You dream in a rhythmic
rise and fall
unaware of the
violence in your veins -
Then
palpitations drum the ears
of nature -
A barn owl's hooting is bent
by the roar -
Bells are choked in the steeple's
throat by decibels -
A trout's splash leaves a ring
of silent surprise -
The constant hum of horse power
has replaced the diminishing
clip-clop -

Saturday night used to end with
lights out -
lights on -
windows open -
You could hear the
windows open -
Not now -
Most stay shut -
The noise . . . .

LEAVES

I have seen the Severn
full of ships
launched by a sealed stem
and the stern wind -
Watched them sail
from peerless trees
of beech, birch and oak;
alder and ash;
float frost-red
and autumn cold
into the sea's sunken eye,
then die, gloriously.

The death of the year.

'. . . and man made God in his own image . . . '

There is a book that is black.
Most pages are white - holy white.
Some are yellow - yellow with sage.
God loves yellow, black and white folk.
No joke!

There are books called 'Holy Books'.
A 'Holy Book' has pages of rice paper.
My 'Holy Book' weighs sixteen ounces.
My 'Holy Book' has sixteen ounces of rice paper.

Sixteen ounces of rice must feed
six people, victims of floods,
famines, fears, earthquakes, wars
and withering disease, for one day only.
If they can get it!

'Half a pound of twopenny rice'
no longer stands,
but if it did,
it would feed three people for one day
in far too many lands.
If they can get it!

Half a pound of rice in a tin
with milk and sugar is ambrosia
for you, me and the gods.
We can get it!

'Trust in the Lord and do good;
so shalt thou dwell in the land,
and verily shalt thou be fed.'
If they can get it!

'Delight thyself also in the Lord;
and he shall give thee
the desires of thy heart.'
If they can get it!

'I have been young and now am old;
yet have I not seen the righteous forsaken
nor his seed begging bread.'
     Happy are the blind for they shall see nothing.

'Behold the fowls of the air: for they sow not,
neither do they reap, nor gather into barns;
yet your heavenly father feedeth them.
Are ye not much better than they?'
     Yes, sixteen ounces of rice better,
     if they can get it!

'Therefore take no thought, saying,
What shall we eat? or what shall we drink?
or, wherewithal shall we be clothed?
But seek ye first the Kingdom of God
and his righteousness; and all these things
shall be added unto you.'
     Happy are the blind for they shall see nothing.

There is a book that is black -
Obviously black.
Most pages are white -
Pestilent pale.
Some are yellow -
The pallor of death.
God loves yellow, black and white folk.
     No joke!

Your God must eat your words.
People need rice,
     not rice paper words.

PENNY WISE — POUND FOOLISH

It happened on the London to Brighton run . . . . .
Security Express van . . . . .
Nearly half a million in used notes!

They stopped in a Croydon lay-by;
'Call of nature', it was said.
A matter of inconvenience because,
as the guards stepped out,
in stole the shot-gun men
from a big maroon van,
followed by a green one,
and three getaway cars!

'They were seen to drive off fast',
the newspapers said, 'heading south,
and last night the guards were still
at the police station.'

Were they being told,
I wondered,
that if you look after
the pennies,
the pounds
do *not* look after themselves . . . . . ?

DIARY

If you know your name was written
in a certain someone's diary
this year,
and no Christmas card arrives,
you can be sure that in the
certain someone's diary
for next year,
your name will not appear.
A possible remedy
then for the card that never came,
is to send a diary
having written in your
name.
Or,
send a New Year's card
and
hit their conscience hard.
Or,
if you never want to see
the certain someone
again,   refrain
from writing their name
in your new diary.